Everything I Needed to Know About Parenting I Learned in Prison

TALES OF A CORRECTIONAL OFFICER

Leslie G. Nelson

Jill,

Thanks so much
for the inspiration you
have been not only
to my kids —
but me
as well
Leslie!

Book Layout ©2013 BookDesignTemplates.com

Everything I Needed to Know About Parenting I Learned in
Prison/Leslie G. Nelson —1st ed.
ISBN 978-1493782376

For Ammon, Caleb, Vienna, Brigham and Peter
You are the lights that shine on my dark days.

Contents

Before Children, There were Inmates

.

"UNLESS YOU DO SOMETHING deliberately to change it, you will become the same kind of parent that your parents are." Years ago, a wise high school teacher said these words and it has changed my life.

I started thinking: What kind of parent did I want to be? What did I like about my parents' methods? What would I like to do differently? I began to study parents and children. I watched them in the grocery stores and department stores. I watch them still.

As I was forming some ideas about parenting, my "training" took an unexpected turn. I started working as a corrections officer in a men's prison. First, I want you to understand that I am not the "stereotypical" female prison guard, whatever that may be for you. Let's just say that when I got the job my friends teased me about being a female Barney Fife! So how did a naïve small-town girl like me end up working in prison?

Well, I was at one of those crossroads in life and my wheels were spinning. I was twenty-two. I had recently returned from an LDS (Mormon) mission and I was working as a cashier in a mom-and-pop grocery store, which equaled "no future." I didn't have a car or any prospects. I needed a change, but what? Then my old friend and roommate, Charice Hunt, called and said, "They're hiring here! Come join me!"

"Ummm, no thanks. You work in prison. I could never do that!"

She laughed. "Don't worry, its just like babysitting grown men."

Sure, whatever you say, I thought. But she was right! So began what could be called the world's most unique parenting training course. You may be skeptical. How could being a correctional officer train someone for parenting? I know it sounds crazy, but there are some techniques for dealing with inmates that translate nicely to parenting. By the time I traded my uniform and badge for maternity clothes, I had changed, and the influence has carried over into the way I parent.

My husband and I have five children now. I don't claim to be an expert on parenting. I am still learning, and my ideas are still changing. That is how it should be. Parenting is not just about how we shape the children we have been blessed with, but how they shape and change us as well.

Leslie

[1]

Teamwork: Let's March

BEFORE ONE CAN WORK in prison, some training is required. New hires attend a Correctional Officer Training Academy (COTA). This eight week course is modeled after the police academy. At COTA, the prospective officers are trained in rules, inmate games, weapons, and marching.

My job was in a small prison town. You know the kind of town I'm talking about, right? Where everyone in town is either working at the prison, related to someone working at the prison, or related to an inmate. For our academy, they refurbished an abandoned school. We slept and ate there, but mostly we sat in class for long hours and learned the prison rules. We also learned about prison culture. I'll explain more about that later. Long periods of listening to lectures were broken up by marching. Marching in formation, working on crisp left and right turns, stopping and starting at the same time . . .

The marching was a mystery to me. I suspected, and I was right, that after COTA graduation, we would never have to march again. What was the point? I wondered. Our teachers told us it was to teach discipline and teamwork. Still, it seemed more likely that it was just a way to kill time, as in, "Hey, we ran out of material for today, so we'll just make them march!"

Looking back, I think it was a little bit of both. I admit the concept of teamwork is an important one in prison. It is very much an us-versus-them mentality. If you disagree with another officer, you put on your best poker face and deal with it later—privately. To show any sort of division in front of the inmates would be like tossing a wounded fish to a piranha.

Likewise, the inmates have a team mentality. They may fear one another, hate one another, even try to kill one another, but they do not snitch. In inmate culture, snitching is the worst thing one can do. To do so is almost certain death.

Teamwork applies to parenting as well, though fortunately, it is not the same us-versus-them mentality.

Being united in parenting means different things. The first thing that comes to everyone's mind is likely rules and discipline. This is very important. Like inmates, children will sometimes pick up on their parents' division and use it to their own advantage.

I have found that the best way to acquire this unity on rules and discipline is through talking, talking, and more talking. Remember that thing you loved to do with your spouse before you had children and became sleep-deprived zombies? You may be tempted to just do things your way when your spouse is not around. Resist this temptation! Children not only have excellent memories, but they say whatever is on their mind without filtering.

Take this for example. A couple was not in complete agreement about a shopping matter—the wife loved See's Candies, but the husband thought it was overpriced. So one day, the wife took their child to See's candy store. She disposed of the wrappers and thought that since the child was too young to know where they went, they were home free. That is until the little girl, when asked about her day, proudly told her dad, "We went to the black-and-white store." Busted. He immediately recognized this to mean the black-and-white tiled linoleum of See's.

Another aspect of working as a team is the marriage relationship. It is stressful for children to see their parents argue. I'm not suggesting that parents should never disagree with one another in front of their children; if handled properly, this can be a great teaching moment. We can show children how to resolve disagreements if we are good role models.

Unfortunately, sometimes we adults need some work in this area. It is possible to disagree respectfully, and only you know if you are able to do that. Couples who struggle with this should resolve their differences in private. My definition of "respectful disagreement" is no name calling, no raised voices, just calm conversation. This is not so say that you won't get irritated, but don't yell. I know this is easier said than done, as the old cliché goes, but if you cannot have a respectful disagreement, it's best to resolve differences privately. I also use the concept of teamwork with my children. No, I don't make them march in straight lines, but as they have gotten older, I've encouraged them to treat one another respectfully in a sort of "us-verses-the world" mentality. The world can be an unkind place, but home should be a place where you know you will be treated kindly, even by your siblings. Of course, I also use "teamwork" to explain why everyone needs to help with chores. I want my kids to know that it is not my job as their mother to be their maid and butler. I also want them to take some ownership in helping make our home run smoothly not just because I asked them to, but because it benefits the whole family when we all pitch in. I have to admit, though, that there are days when the thought of seeing them march in perfect obedience to my commands sounds tempting.

[2]

Firm, Fair and Consistent

BEFORE ONE CAN WORK in prison, there is much to learn. Policies, procedures, do's, and especially the don'ts! Much of our classroom time at COTA was spent on these issues. We spent long hours learning rules and regulations, but we also had a little fun along the way. One boredom buster was learning how to apply handcuffs. Naturally, we practiced on each other. I didn't care much for wearing them, but it was fun to cuff my friends. We also practiced pat-downs on one another. That was a little too close for comfort and provoked a lot of nervous laughter.

The most influential lesson I learned in the academy was, "Firm, fair, consistent." This was drilled into us daily, hourly, and for good reason. This is an essential tool for correctional officers. Some inmates are like master chess players. They have a lot of time on their hands and they entertain themselves by studying officers and looking for any weakness they can exploit. Weakness or inconsistencies are exactly the kind of thing they look for. Unfairness? Well, for some inmates, the mere fact that you are an officer makes you inherently unfair. You can't get around that one in their minds, but you may need to prove to your superiors that you have been fair to all.

Firm, fair, and consistent applies just as much to parents. As a young mom, I would sometimes get frustrated with my children and think, "They are not listening to me!" But when I took time to reflect on my own actions, I would often find that I had not been firm, fair, and (the biggest culprit) consistent.

Inmates and children are very astute and can spot inconsistencies. For them, inconsistencies are like loopholes for getting away with something.

So what does it mean to be firm, fair, and consistent?

It means that you have rules, everyone knows what the rules are, and the rules are enforced (all the time, even when you are tired). That last part has been the hardest for me. As any mom knows, being tired comes with the territory!

The rules should be reasonable, and, when possible, agreed upon by everyone involved. In prison, we did not get the consent of all the inmates on the rules. If they had a vote, they would choose to have more pornography (yes, that is against the rules), alcohol, and drugs. In a family, however, it can be beneficial to have children help decide on the rules.

The rules apply equally to all. In prison, we can't let one inmate have certain privileges that another does not receive simply because we don't want to deal with the argument or whining that will ensue. And yet, as parents, aren't we all tempted to do that sometimes?

Perhaps the hardest part is consistency. As parents, when we are tired, stressed, sick, or simply distracted we can slip on the consistency. If you look around, you will see parents struggling with this all the time.

"Mommy, I want candy."

"No, honey."

"Plea-a-s-s-s-e!"

"No."

"Waaaaaaaaaaaaaaaaaaaaaaaahhhhhhhhhhhhhhhhhhh!"

The parent doesn't want to draw the attention of every shopper in the store, so she will give the candy to the child to quiet them. I have seen this happen many times over the years. The problem is the child has learned that when Mom says "no," she doesn't really mean it. Thus, the next time she says "no," the child is less inclined to listen.

In dog training, they emphasize that the owners need training, not the dogs. So it is with parents. In Spanish, they don't have a word for "spoiled," but instead they say, mal creado, meaning,"badly raised." If our child screams for a candy bar in the store because we have given into them, who is at fault? This is why firm, fair, and consistent is so important.

There are two things that have helped me in those kinds of situations. First, I consider my words before I speak, and once you've said it, you have to follow through. Don't say "We'll go home" if you still have shopping to do. The other thing that helps is validation. I say, "Yes, that candy bar looks really good. I understand why you want it, but we haven't had lunch yet, so no candy bar." Then I try to distract them with something else. We often hear about kids acting out to get attention. Validation is a wonderful form of attention; knowing that we are heard and understood is something we all crave.

Another place where consistency frequently fails is in the one-two-three method of discipline. Mom says, "Johnny, put that toy back and come over here."

Johnny feigns deafness.

"Johnny, I'm going to count to three. One, two . . ."

Long pause as Johnny's pretend-deafness continues.

"Two and a half. . ." pause, then the exasperated mother walks over, throws the toy in the cart, and pulls Johnny along.

Again, what has Johnny learned?

Personally, I don't care for the one-two-three method. Even if it were used consistently, I want my children to respond the first time they are asked. Counting gives them permission to ignore you for at least the count of two. It doesn't mean that I expect them to jump like well-trained soldiers when I bark a command, but I don't want them to wait for two and a half either. I believe that respect flows both ways. I try to respond to their requests promptly and teach them to do the same for me.

When we use these principles, our children will not only be more obedient, but happier and more secure. And aren't those things we all hope for?

[3]

Inmate Games: It's Not Monopoly

INMATES HAVE A LOT OF TIME on their hands. Did your grandmother ever tell you the old adage, "Idle hands are the devil's workshop"? This is never truer than in prison. Inmates use their idle hands and idle minds to play games. Almost all inmates do it. No, they're not playing Monopoly. They actually play endless variations of the same game. It doesn't have a name, but if it did, it would be "Trip Up the Guards." In other words, they entertain themselves by trying to make the officers mess up.

The stakes in this game can be very high. The higher the stakes, the more interesting it is for the inmates. Their ultimate goal is for the officer to wear prison garb and wave good-bye to their family through a chain-link fence. The inmates would to settle for getting an officer fired, though. They have other goals with female officers, as you can well imagine.

Inmates know that if they ask an officer to bring in drugs for them the officer will refuse. So they try to lure the officer into a trap where they can't refuse. This is where the game begins.

First, inmates try to get an officer to break "little" rules. Things that "don't matter." For example, there was one inmate who was very polite and kind to me. One day he handed me a piece of paper. I took it discretely just in case he was trying to do the unthinkable—snitch. When I realized the note was a love poem, I let him know that if it happened again he would be written up. Writing love notes to officers is against the rules and he knew it. He avoided me after that, no more polite conversation. He wasn't heartbroken; he had probably just moved on to a new target.

If an inmate can get an officer to break a "little" rule, they try for something bigger, then bigger. Slowly, they "reel" the officer in. Eventually, the goal is to get the officer to do something they would not want their superiors (or their fellow officers for that matter) to know about. Then the real fun begins (at least from the inmate's perspective). "I want you to meet my friend Bob, and he is going to give you some drugs." When the officer says no, the inmate says, "Do it or I will tell the sergeant that you . . ." At this point, an officer may feel that he or she has "no choice" and the trap is sprung.

With female officers, they turn on the charm. They must read romance novels, because some of them are very good at it! As female officers, we sometimes lamented that guys in the real world never treated us as well as the inmates did. I used their efforts to be charming to my advantage. Since they were trying to get on my good side, they almost always did what I asked them to do. One time, four inmates knelt down simultaneously and asked me to marry them. It was hilarious. They were joking, but if I had shown any interest, they would have followed through until they got what they wanted and I got fired.

In the Academy, our instructors warned us repeatedly about inmate games. They told us that four people out of our class of thirty-four would most likely get fired for "inappropriate relations" with inmates. We were amazed and in denial. Not us! But sure enough, in the year I was there, one of my classmates was arrested for bringing in drugs, and two female officers were fired for having sex with inmates.

But what do inmate games have to do with parenting? Well, as a new mother I was taught, "Don't hold the baby too much or you will spoil him." The idea seems to be that we need to "show 'em who's the boss" right from the beginning, as if babies are as conniving as inmates.

I wonder where that idea came from. It is not the norm in other cultures. Imagine for a moment that you are a baby. You depend on others to do everything for you. If you are cold, hungry, or scared, you need someone to assist you. How do you communicate your needs to the people you depend on? You cry and they come. Great, so far so good, right? But then sometimes you cry and they don't come. What do you feel?

The philosophy of spoiling depends on well-developed powers of reasoning: "If I cry, I'll get my way." Little babies can't reason at that level yet. They are not capable of being manipulative or playing games. They simply need to have their needs met, and they only have one way to communicate their needs.

With my first two children, I hadn't put this all together yet, so I did what all my friends were doing. I put them to bed by letting them "cry it out" and I tried not to hold them "too much." Later, I read about attachment parenting and liked those ideas better. So with my next babies I picked them up often. In fact, I carried them in a sling so I could hold them more often. Another parent once said to me, "Why do you always carry her? How is she going to learn to walk?"

That child, and all the others, learned to walk just fine, and none of them became spoiled. If you knew my children, you would not be able to tell which ones I let "cry it out" and which ones were carried in a sling. So perhaps there are not long-lasting effects of either method. I can't say for sure about the children, but I know that attachment parenting was a much healthier for me. And besides, it's so true that the time passes all too quickly.

What about the terrible twos? Okay, this is the age where I think children can become spoiled. Tantrums are an understandable reaction to the frustration that a child surely feels, but giving into them does not help either the child or the parent. It is hard to know the right answer. With my child, I sometimes would just let him cry it out a bit. Sometimes I would talk to him soothingly and help him begin to develop the vocabulary for how he is feeling. I said, "I know you are mad. You are really, really mad." Or, "I'm sorry you are so sad right now."

I believe one of the big reasons for the tantrums is a child's inability to communicate their needs and wants, and also their inability to understand why their wants are not always met. When my daughter was two, she went through a period where she threw the most horrible tantrums. We nicknamed her "Firecracker" because she was so explosive. I tried ignoring her, putting her in time out, talking to her, and though it was tempting, I never gave in to her. Still, nothing seemed to help diffuse her or prevent the tantrums.

Then I started learning American Sign Language (ASL). Just for fun, I started teaching her some signs. That was the beginning of the end of the tantrums. ASL gave her a way to communicate until her verbal skills improved. She's a teenager now, and she still loves sign language. Of course, every child is different. My youngest child knew some signs, and that skill did not keep him from having a tantrum when he didn't get his way. If only children were "one size fits all" or "one method fits all."

The important thing is that inmates manipulate and play games, children don't. Sometimes we may need to be a detective to find the cause of the tantrums, but I believe if we are firm, fair, and consistent, we can shower our children with love without the fear that they will become spoiled.

[4]

The Power of the Word

ALL JOBS HAVE THEIR pros and cons, and working as a correctional officer is no different, only the stakes can be higher. In COTA, the instructors try to prepare you for the atmosphere and culture of prison. They teach this with lectures and role-playing.

My friend, Charice, the one who encouraged me to work in prison, told me a story about her COTA training. One day, a "game" was introduced with the goal of helping to prepare officers for being yelled at by inmates. So the cadets were paired up. One by one, the pairs came forward and took turns standing toe-to-toe and yelling obscenities at one another.

Charice had a different idea. When it was her turn, she walked up to the front with her partner and listened while her partner yelled profanities at her. Then it was Charice's turn. She looked at her partner and asked in a calm voice, "Were you in too much of a hurry to comb your hair this morning?

You really should have made time to shower at least. Do you ever iron your uniform?" And so forth.

Afterwards, the teachers asked Charice's partner what she thought about this unique approach. Her partner said, "It was terrible! Even though I knew she didn't mean it, it made me feel so bad. I would much rather have her yell and swear at me."

This story has obvious ties to parenting. As parents, do we appreciate the power of the language? Not just the things that we as parents say, but what siblings say to one another?

I don't allow my children to speak to each other unkindly. Unkind words are not only damaging to relationships but to self-esteem. Some people say, "Kids will be kids." Yes, and puppies will be puppies. They will pee in the house and chew up your shoes until you teach them a better way. Our children will fight and quarrel, but that doesn't mean we need to accept it. We need to try to teach them better relationship skills. How do we teach them? I believe it begins with us—the parents—with our example and our self-talk. When I hear someone who is critical of others, I wonder what their self-talk is like. In other words, how do they talk to themselves. There is wisdom in the saying, "Woe unto the neighbor of the man who loves his neighbor as his self when he hates himself." We are harder on ourselves than anyone else. If all we are hearing all day are awful messages about ourselves, from ourselves, how can we then show love to those around us? You know your faults better than most, but you also know what is in your heart—all the good that is there—better than most. Talk to yourself about what a great person you are once in a while!

Next, we need to consider the way we speak to our spouses. Does the way we speak to one another set an example for the children? If not, can we change? Of course we can! Every day is a new opportunity to be better than we were before.

Now, we are ready to consider how we speak to children. As mothers, we are in a position to give orders. It is a necessary part of the job, if you will. "Get dressed. Eat your breakfast. Do your chores. Make your bed. Do your homework. Don't jump on the couch . . ." and so forth. Those things come naturally. Unfortunately, it is not so natural to say, "You are so awesome. Thank you for making your bed. Good job!" We have to make a conscious effort to do those things. Some parents are very good at that, while some of us can improve.

Finally, how do the children speak to one another? They are young, and as such, their patience is still developing, their tempers need toning, and their words may need softening. Even if you have been careful to set a fine example with your spouse, they pick up words and attitudes from TV, school, and other influences. Our job is to help them develop patience, control their tempers, and bridle their tongues. I deal with this in different ways depending on the situation. Usually, just a comment is enough to make them stop. Sometimes they need a mediator to help them see one another's position and to express their own in better ways. If the mediating is not enough, then sometimes I will make them work together—ideally serve one another. For example, they have jobs around the house that they do, so I will make them help one another with their chores. You love those you serve.

The world can be an ugly, competitive place. Our homes should not be. Our homes can and should be the place where we can be loved and supported even when we do dumb things.

[5]

Riots, Mutiny and Family Feuds

INMATES USED TO ASK me, "Aren't you afraid working here?" I would just laugh and reply, "No. When I am here at work, I know there is always another officer watching my back. It is much scarier to go home to my dark house at night. But I have a dog—a vicious dog—with large, sharp teeth." They would always laugh at this.

What I told them was partially true. I did feel confident that another officer was always watching, and if something happened, there is a team of highly trained officers (with tear gas and weapons) that could be called upon. One thing that did make me nervous was the possibility of a prison riot. I spent a lot of time wondering what would be the best time for the inmates to riot if they so desired, and what signs an officer should look for. While I was in the academy, they warned us, "If you are ever in a riot or hostage situation, get on the floor! We don't negotiate; we'll come in with weapons blasting." That was not comforting.

There was one inmate, a large, quiet African American man, who worked in the kitchen. I don't think he ever said more than two or three words to me, just "good morning" or "thank you." One day, though, he quietly said to me, "If anything ever goes down here, don't try to be a hero. Get yourself into an empty cell and lock yourself in until it is over because these guys mean business." I thought that sounded like good advice. I was on my guard for the next week or so wondering if he knew something was coming.

We did have a couple small riots during the time I worked at the prison. During the first one, I was working in the Main Control Room. That means I was in charge of the doors leading into and out of the yard and the gate. I administered the keys and radios, and when the small riot broke out, I was the center of communication.

I do not multi-task well, so when the door alarms suddenly buzzed because officers wanted to come into the control room and get rifles, the radio was squawking, the phone was ringing, and my anxiety level exploded like a space rocket.

To further complicate things, the warden called and demanded an explanation of what was going on in the yard. All I could tell him was, "I'll let you know when I get some info, sir." He took that about as well as you would expect; in other words, he made inmate language look tame.

I let the officers into the control room, and they grabbed shotguns and went out into the yard. Officers do not carry weapons routinely because it is too dangerous. After all, on an ordinary day, you are constantly outnumbered by inmates, but we do have the weapons available for emergencies.

The riot was quelled quickly, and afterwards a "what we did well and what we could do better next time" meeting was held. My stomach was a churning mess, so I chugged Mylanta straight from the bottle much to the amusement of my co-workers.

Fortunately as parents, we don't have riots of that magnitude, but we can experience the occasional mutiny. The difference is that in a riot, the inmates fight officers, one another, and destroy property, but in a mutiny, the inmates simply all band together against the captain.

In this case, working as an officer has taught me what not to do. Coming in with a show of force and ready to use it is not the best scenario for homes and families. We have better tools at our discretion.

One of those tools is the age-old thing called "compromise." I relearned this skill in a later job working with at-risk youth. As I mentioned before, I am still learning and refining my parenting skills. I wish I had started using this tool earlier. In my work, they call it "Basket B."There are actually three baskets: A, B, and C. Basket A is the adult's will; this is for when the stakes are high, like when a child is running into the street. No compromise here—the parents' judgment rules. Basket C is the child's will. Sometimes it is beneficial to let the child choose. Basket B is for both. This is where compromise comes in.

Basket B is a wonderful refinement of compromise. First, the parent explains the situation to the child and asks the child how they think the problem would be solved. For example, once my seven-year-old son was refusing to eat dinner. My old style would have been to say, "That's fine, son, but there isn't anything else to eat. You can go to bed hungry if that is your choice."

But I decided to try Basket B. It looked something like this:

"Son, I understand that you don't want what I made for dinner, but I don't have time to make anything else. What do you think we should do?"

Because he was so young, he didn't have a ready solution, but he told me he really wanted macaroni and cheese.

Asking your child how he or she would solve the problem is powerful because it makes them feel valued as a family member, and it helps them learn to make decisions and think for themselves. This in turn helps build confidence, but if they don't have a suggestion, you can offer something and ask them what they think.

"Son, we already have dinner ready for tonight, but how about you eat this and I will make macaroni and cheese tomorrow? Does that sound all right?"

His little face beamed with delight and he agreed to eat the dinner I had made. I admit that I wondered at the time if I was setting myself up for a request for macaroni and cheese every other day, or some other sort of mutiny. That didn't happen though. He ate dinner that night, and macaroni and cheese the next night, and there were no further food issues for a while.

That went smoothly—beginner's luck, perhaps. If he had said he wanted to eat macaroni and cheese every night, then we would have had to continue our negotiations. What I appreciate the most about Basket B is that both the parent and the child should be happy with the solution.

I tried a slightly different version of this with my teenagers when we were preparing to move. Packing and cleaning for a move is a huge job and I needed their help. It seemed reasonable to let them have some say in what they wanted to do. I firmly believe people and children work harder when they are doing something they want to do. I reasoned that while my teens surely would have preferred spending time with their friends to packing and cleaning, having some choice in which task they undertook might help their motivation. So each morning after breakfast I would say, "What do you want to do to help with the moving effort today?"

Remember, in Basket B both the parent and the child have to be happy, so if my son offered a solution that was not satisfying to me, I would say something like, "That sounds good, and what else?" Then he would offer to do a little more, and so the conversation went until we were both happy.

Basket B has worked out to be a wonderful tool, but if it ever fails and we have a mutiny in our home-making the kids walk the plank is still an option.

[6]

Hootch and Shanks

INMATES ARE VERY RESOURCEFUL, but not in healthy ways. They have been known to hoard kitchen scraps like bread and fruit to make an alcoholic beverage called "Hootch." Worse, they find scraps of metal and sharpen them into makeshift knives called "shanks." For this reason, they are only allowed to use plastic silverware. Once when I was working, an inmate was killed in some gang rivalry. The murder weapon? The sharp edges of a shovel.

Naturally, there are rules against this sort of thing, but inmates are notorious for not adhering to the rules. Officers conduct routine cell searches for this very reason. In a cell search, the inmate is required to stand outside of the cell, or he may not even be in the area. The officers, always two at a time, go in and search the cell inch by inch for any contraband. Contraband, of course, is anything against the rules, which includes food, pornography, shanks, etc. One time, officers found a list of names and credit card numbers in an inmate's cell. Obviously, that was confiscated!

Children are also very resourceful also, but fortunately not with the same malicious intent as inmates. To a child, any bed, couch, or chair is a mini-trampoline. Any surface more than twelve inches off the floor is a jumping-off point, and any stick, branch, or cardboard scrap becomes a sword. These activities are just fun, but they can have unanticipated consequences.

An old friend of mine, Todd, told me a story when he and his brothers had been jumping off a shed roof on their property when they were younger. Unfortunately, his brother slipped and fell. As he slid down the roof, a nail sliced his stomach wide open. Slowly he made his way to the house, hunched over and bleeding. His mother, who had seen a lot of injuries by having boys, didn't even look up from her mopping and said, "Go back outside and don't drip blood on the floor." There's a practical mom for you. Of course, once she realized the gravity of the situation, she responded appropriately.

In prison, there are many, many volumes of rules and regulations; the main purpose of these volumes is to keep the officers and the inmates safe. Officers, of course, cannot possibly remember all the rules, but they remember their favorites. Probably the most frequently used is "disobeying a direct order."

As a parent, I decided it would be better to keep things simple. After all, what good are long lists of family rules if the children can't even read yet?

So instead of numerous rules such as:

Don't jump on the bed.

Don't jump off the bed.

Don't climb on the table and jump off.

Don't play with knives.

Don't throw rocks.

Don't . . .

Don't . . .

We have one rule that covers all of the above: "Proper Use." I explain to the children that when things are used in a manner different than what they were intended, property can be damaged, or worse, people can get hurt. Therefore, when they do something inappropriate like jumping on the couch, I just look at them and say, "Proper Use." They know just what I mean.

We have a one rule for teasing too. We are a family that loves to tease and joke with each other. With children, however, sometimes teasing can get out of hand. Our solution is a one-size-fits-all rule—both people must be having fun. If one person doesn't like it, it must stop.

Success in teaching our children to respect themselves, others, and property will protect them from ever having to learn volumes of prison rules—unless they want to learn them as an officer.

[7]

Solitary Confinement

PROGRESSIVE DISCIPLINE is used in prison. Correction starts as a warning, then a ticket, and gradually increases. This works well with children too. In prison, one of the more serious punishments is solitary confinement.

When I worked at the prison, there was a small solitary confinement area; it was only about ten cells. Inmates in this area are only allowed to come out of their cells for showers or for recreation time (rec). Rec is one hour in a caged space about ten-by-ten feet, but it was fresh air. In order to leave his cell, an inmate must put his hands through a small rectangular hole in the door that was designed for this purpose. He is handcuffed, and only then is the door opened.

One day the entire prison lost power. The back-up generator immediately came on, so the power failure should not have been a problem. However, prison doors have electronic locks, so as the power clicked off and the generator clicked on, all the doors became unlocked. Ten of the worst inmates in our prison could open their own doors. An officer grabbed a shotgun and stepped into the hallway. He pumped it, racking a shell into the chamber, which made that very recognizable cla-click sound. All ten doors immediately clicked shut!

Parents also use solitary confinement; we just call it "room time" or "time out." I think every parent has used this at one time or another. If you haven't, your children just aren't old enough.

I don't need to use room time often, but I do use it as necessary. One instance that comes to mind was when my twelve-year-old son sassed me. I can't remember what he said, but it was dripping with sarcasm. This was a first, and I was furious. I didn't want to say anything that I would regret (which is not to say that I have never done that; I just caught myself that time). So I sent him to his room.

After a reasonable cooling-off period, I invited him to talk to me. I told him, "You are welcome to disagree with me, but you will do it respectfully. I do not speak to you with disrespect and sarcasm, and you will not do it to me. Understand?" Then I grounded him from the computer and video games for a week, because I wanted to make a point.

Respect for yourself, others, and property is very important in our home. Without it, everything else begins to unravel. I try not to overuse the solitary confinement consequence though. Usually, other methods are more effective and meaningful. As my husband often reminds me, our job as parents is not simply to make our children obey, but to teach them how to be responsible adults.

[8]

Dreams:Theirs and Ours

RECREATION TIME IS WHEN inmates come out of their cells, exercise, hang out, talk to their friends, etc. Officers are expected to mingle with the population during this time and maintain a presence. One day during rec, I stopped to talk to a couple inmates and one of them, hoping to get some kind of reaction from me, asked, "Did you dream about me last night?"

I smiled. "Yes, as a matter of fact I did." Suddenly, I felt a dozen pairs of eyes on me. I not only had his attention, but that of everyone standing within earshot. Pleased with my audience, I continued.

"I had a dream that I was working on the perimeter again."

The perimeter is one of the jobs where officers drive slowly, no faster than ten miles an hour, around the perimeter of the prison. They inspect the fence for any flaws and the sand traps for footprints. They have a shotgun and a handgun to be used as needed.

"In my dream, I was driving along and I saw an inmate climbing down the outside of the fence. I shouted, 'Halt', three times, but the guy didn't stop. So I shot him . . . When I ran over to the body, it was you. Sorry about that, but you should have stopped when I asked you to."

Laughter exploded around us. "Man, she really dissed you!" That inmate and his friends never made lewd remarks to me again.

Like that inmate, parents have certain expectations and dreams for our children that don't always work out as planned. Quite often those dreams are influenced by our own unfulfilled goals and dreams. Sometimes they are simply dreams about the kind of parent we want to be and the way our children will behave.

My children all seemed determined from the beginning to tell me to keep my plans to myself. Well, not all of them, but enough. For example, I love to sing. One of my dreams was to sing lullabies to my babies. I was mesmerized with the idea, but when my first child was fussing and I started to sing, he cried harder. I tried different songs, but the only thing I accomplished was to infuriate him more. When I stopped, he calmed, so I quit singing for a few months (sometimes I'm a slow learner). Later, I tried again. He reached up and put his hand over my mouth! I surrendered and stopped trying to sing to him.

When I had my second child, I tried again but had similar disappointing results. Sheesh. Even today it is a joke in our family. If I start singing my favorite Broadway tune, "I am Don Quixote, the Lord of La Mancha" (at the top of my lungs, which is the only way to sing it), the whole family gangs up on me to make me stop. Spoil sports!

There were other dashed dreams as well. For example, my dream to teach them to speak Spanish, which I had the wonderful opportunity to learn and wanted to pass on, is still unrealized.

Another disappointment came when I signed a couple of the older kids up for a program called "Destination Imagination." It's an after-school program created to help children learn to be leaders. They are organized in teams and they are given challenges to complete. For example, a challenge could be: build a structure that will be tested against two forces at the same time. They have weekly practice challenges and they go to competitions and compete against other teams. I thought it would be a terrific experience for them. When they both informed me that they were bored and wanted to drop out, I was dismayed, not only because I thought it was such a great opportunity, but it is a team effort and I didn't want them to let down their team. I didn't think boredom was a reasonable excuse to quit either. I did the best mom-guilt-trip I could muster. Their dad tried too, but to no avail. In the end, they still wanted to quit. I realized that if their heart wasn't in it, they would not be able to give their best effort to the team, so I gave them permission to quit. Their team did fine without them; they won the state competition and went to the national competition. I was thrilled for the team, but still bummed that my kids didn't share the dream.

I realize these are minor things, but having experienced them, I dreaded the day when they started dating, and, heaven forbid, when they get married. Will I be disappointed again when they choose a spouse who is different than I would have chosen? And what about school? I always wanted to go to college. I planned for college. I had the grades, but not the money. Naturally, I want my children to go to college, but will they? So many other dreams, waiting to be fulfilled or deflated.

I have to say that even though some of my dreams for my children have been unrealized, they have also surprised and pleased me in so many other ways. As they grow and develop, their talents are becoming evident, and certain personality traits are beginning to emerge. Sometimes it feels like parenting is a kaleidoscope. As you hold it to the light and twist it, amazing patterns emerge. You can't control the patterns, but each one is beautiful and leaves you wanting more.

Now I think of my dreams for my children not so much in details as in "they will do this" or "they will do that," but that each child is a kaleidoscope of possibilities, and my part is to show them light and love then enjoy the beautiful patterns as they emerge.

[9]

A Pinch of Kindness:
A Little Goes A Long Way

INMATE BANNER, (name changed to protect the innocent .
. . um, well, to protect the inmate), was one of the crankiest
people I met in prison. His vocabulary consisted solely of
swear words. Anyone who spoke to him for any reason was
greeted with a stream of foul language. This was interesting
to me because most inmates upon realizing that I didn't
swear promptly cleaned up their language, which was all
part of the inmate games, but it was still a nice gesture.
Banner was different; his colorful vocabulary knew no boun-
daries.

In addition to his temper, I had noticed something else
about Banner—his hair. He had the most incredible hair. It
was long, well past his shoulders, thick, straight, and shiny
much like Native Americans have been blessed with. If that
was not enough, it had natural brown streaks among the
dark black color—gorgeous hair. I was so envious; I still am.
One day I decided to tell him—a sort of sociology experi-

ment. If I told the grumpiest inmate that I liked his hair, what would happen?

It was during count time. Count time is just what it sounds like. Certain times of the day are set aside to count the inmates and make sure none have escaped. So I opened his cell door with the key and said, "Banner?" He answered with his usual expletives. I almost lost my nerve, but I said, "I just wanted to tell you I love your hair. If you ever cut it, will you give it to me for a wig?" He didn't answer, but he smiled. No barrage of swear words, so I took that as a good sign and left to continue my rounds.

An amazing thing happened. He never swore at me again. He didn't try to take advantage of my kindness either. If I said, "Good morning Banner," he responded with a simple, "Good morning," with no four-letter condiments. I could hardly believe it.

I learned something from that experience with Banner about the power of human kindness. Given the prison environment, I imagine it had been a long time since anyone had complimented him or even been kind, especially since his behavior didn't welcome it.

Children, of course, thrive on praise and attention also. I remember a time when my husband and I were having trouble with one of our sons. At the time we only had three children (two boys, one girl) and the middle child was acting out against his mild-mannered big brother. Let me be more specific: son number two seemed to delight in beating up son number one. My older son's only response was to cry. He made no attempt to defend himself.

We did all the usual things, scoldings, time outs, etc., that parents do to try to curb these sorts of behaviors. But nothing worked. We were seriously considering teaching the older child to defend himself. Then we prayed about it and an impression came to me: my younger son wanted more attention.

I give him plenty of attention, I thought. But the impression wouldn't go away.

"He doesn't think so."

The implication was that it didn't matter what I thought, but what my son felt. So I started an effort to give him more attention throughout the day, not when he was misbehaving but other times. Just like Inmate Banner, my younger son's response was dramatic and welcome.

Many years have passed since then, but whenever this son would act out, I made more of an effort to give him positive attention. It worked so well that I have tried it with the difficult adults in my life, and ninety-nine percent of the time the results are the same: dramatic and pleasing. It seems that no matter what our age, we all thrive on a little kindness, attention, and sincere flattery.

[10]

Captivity vs. Choice

ONE DAY DURING REC time, I struck up a conversation with Inmate Smith who was standing outside his cell. He mentioned that he was going to be released soon. He had been in prison, or as the inmates say, he had been "down," for twenty years. I thought he must be thrilled and told him so. His response was surprisingly frank. "No, I'm scared."

"Scared? Why?" I asked. He proceeded to tell me about one of his experiences.

For reasons I can't begin to understand, the Department of Corrections once had a program of giving well-behaved inmates a couple days off. As you might guess, they stopped the program when an inmate on furlough committed a worse crime than the one he had been put in prison for. The details are too gruesome to relate here, so I'll just say murder was involved. While this program was still active, Inmate Smith had an opportunity to go on a weekend furlough.

While he was out, a friend showed Smith his new car, and encouraged him to get in and sit in the driver's seat. Smith was sitting alone in the driver's seat when a computerized voice said, "The door is ajar." Smith said he about wet his pants. His friend thought it was hilarious.

Later, Smith went to the store with his sister. He said, "We got our stuff and took it to the cashier, but she didn't ring them up! She just picked them up and put them in the bag. Then she said, 'The total is $63.12.' How could she know what we owed? I started to go off." In inmate lingo, "go off" means to lose your temper and yell, and four-letter words are involved.

He continued, "My sister grabbed my arm and said, 'I'll explain it to you outside.'"

Poor guy. He had never seen barcode scanners. He was used to the old days when the cashier manually typed in each price. Since he didn't understand, and he was accustomed to prison where you constantly have to look out for yourself, he was certain that the cashier was trying to cheat them in some way.

The last straw for Smith came when he went to a department store. A little girl noticed his tattoos. Back then, no one had tattoos except drunken sailors and inmates. So it was rare to see tattoos, and he was sleeved—his tattoos covered both arms from wrist to shoulder. The little girl apparently thought that was really interesting. She stared and stared and then said to her mother, "Look, Mommy! That man has drawings on his arms."

The mother grabbed her daughter's hand and whisked her away. Smith said, "It made me feel really bad." By the end of the weekend, he was exhausted and ready to return to prison.

This story surprised me. The culture shock he had experienced was enough to make him eager to give up something most of us cherish: freedom. Things on the outside had changed so much since he had been incarcerated that he felt like a foreigner in his own country. Or perhaps he felt like a time traveler. Either way it was very unpleasant for him.

Prison life is very structured, so I imagined that this played into his culture shock. Inmates are told when to get up, when to go to bed, when to work, when to have rec, and when and what to eat. Then upon release, they are turned out onto the street with no structure whatsoever. There is no transition time from a very controlled environment to an uncontrolled, sometimes-chaotic one. This is not to say that prison is a pleasant place to be, but humans are creatures of habit.

Between the time-warp factor and the difficult transition from being controlled to freedom, it is no wonder that the recidivism rate is so high. According to Bureau of Justice statistics, in 1994 sixty-seven percent of inmates released were rearrested within three years. Certainly there are other factors, but this merits consideration.

What does this have to do with parenting? Well, isn't our goal to take these beautiful children who come into our lives and help them learn the life skills necessary to go out into the world and be successful? If we examine our habits and culture, are there some things we could change to more ef-fectively prepare our children for their futures?

A friend of mine says that her sixty-year-old mother still tells her to put her coat on. That is sweet and funny; after all, isn't your baby always your baby? It is harmless, and proba-bly just a habit, but the point here is about the way we par-ent. Do our grown children need us to tell them when to put on their coat?

Let's use the coat issue as an example of teaching child-ren to make decisions for themselves. I handle it in different ways depending on the scenario. I ask myself what is the worst thing that could happen if they don't wear their coat, and then I make my decision accordingly.

For example, if it is a fall day and they are walking across the street to their friend's house. I don't even mention the coat. At the worst they will get a little chilly, and then they will arrive at their friend's house. No harm done.

On the other hand, if we are going as a family to watch a football game, odds are good that they are going to get pret-ty chilly and the discomfort will last a few hours. In that sce-nario, I will intervene and ask them to bring a coat. They know they must bring the coat, but they can choose whether or not to put it on.

But at what age do we allow them to start making their own decisions? I think it can and should begin when they are toddlers. Let's talk about a familiar scenario for a mo-ment.

When our children are young, infants to preschool, we worry a lot about spoiling them. We have the idea that too much attention may ruin our child. The commonly held belief when I began my parenting journey was to show the child who is boss. And thus we feel we must always show the child who is in charge.

As they get a little bit older and start to insist on a certain cup, or a certain shirt . . . we say, "No, you will use the cup I gave you." Or, "You will wear this shirt." After all, you're the parent; you're the boss. I wonder if we, like that inmate with the cashier, are working under false assumptions. We assume that the child is trying to be the boss, but what if we try to look at it a different way?

Toddlers are just beginning to explore their world and have a lot of ideas about what they want to do and see. Yet so much of their life is out of their control. Someone tells them when to get up and when to go to bed, what to wear and how to wear it. No, son, you cannot wear those underwear on your head. They are told when to eat and what to eat, when to play and when to take a nap. During playtime they have a little opportunity to make their own choices, but their idea of play is exploring the world around them and then it's, No, honey, leave the TV alone. No, don't play with the dishwasher. No, you can't go outside. No, leave the piles of laundry I'm folding alone.

Can you imagine the frustration? No wonder we have "the terrible twos." Certainly, I don't think they want or need complete freedom at that tender age. But when we try to look at things from their point of view, would it really be so unreasonable to let them use "the blue cup" or have their sandwich cut a certain way? We are not spoiling them by letting them choose what shirt they want to wear or what color cup they want to use. We are giving them their first lessons in decision-making.

Naturally, there are some decisions that children cannot make for themselves. Some things are not safe and sometimes they simply do not have the maturity for certain decisions. Where the line should be drawn will be different for each family. Each child, even within a family, has different capabilities and varying maturity levels. Each parent has different comfort levels. I don't think where one draws the line is as important as the effort to let the children make as many decisions as they are safely able to.

Will we raise spoiled children if we let them make their own decisions as much as possible at a young age? No. Remember Inmate Smith who preferred captivity to freedom? I believe helping our children learn to make decisions for themselves will build confidence and help them become more successful as adults. Isn't that our goal after everything is said and done?

[11]

Living, Breathing, Flesh: Count Time

DURING COUNT TIME, we check to see if all the inmates are "present and accounted for." It's kind of like the roll call we remember from school. During count time, all movement stops. Inmates are sent to their cells. Yes, I used to tell grown men, "Go to your room!"

When inmates are checked at night while they sleep, officers are taught to look for "living, breathing flesh." This evolved due to problems in the past with inmates leaving stuffed pillows under their covers. If we can't see flesh, we have to open the cell door and awaken the inmate. Inmates do not appreciate this, but such is life in prison.

Parents instinctively know about checking for "living, breathing flesh." From the time we bring that first babe into our home we can't stop checking the sleeping baby so make sure he or she is still breathing. My oldest is almost nineteen now and I still make sure all my children are accounted for before I can sleep. It's just what moms do!

Count time is similar to parenting in another way. Almost every time we get in the car, I look in the rearview mirror and do a head check. "One, two, three, four, five . . . okay, we can go." After all, we've all heard stories of moms forgetting their children at the store or the laundromat. One time, I waited for a mom to return after she left one of her children at an activity we had both attended. I never wanted this to happen to me, yet it seems inevitable!

One day when my daughter was fourteen, I took her to visit a friend. The father of the family was our dentist and our kids were friends, so even though we had never been to their house, I felt comfortable with my daughter spending time there.

I worked the overnight shift, so on the day I dropped her off it was my bedtime. I was exhausted, so I didn't bother to go inside and say hello. I just dropped her off. On my way home, I turned my cell phone off because the battery was low. I wanted to save what little battery life remained for an emergency. About twenty minutes later, I arrived home, bleary eyed and ready to get some sleep. My son met me in the driveway and broke the news that I had dropped my daughter off at a stranger's house! I nearly hyperventilated as I rushed back to get her.

I was mortified. How could I have done such a thing? Meanwhile, my daughter was treated very kindly by the family, who had a daughter similar in age to my daughter, just not the one we were looking for. They explained that there was an issue with the addresses and they commonly received the other family's mail. They had never received their visitors though!

When I talk to other moms about this topic, I feel somewhat reassured to hear that everyone has done this at some point whether you have one child or six. Misunderstandings just happen sometimes. My favorite story about this came from my friend, Kristine.

Kristine and her family were moving to another state. She and her husband were driving two different vehicles, and their three children were divided between them. When they stopped for gas, one of her daughters, Brooke, asked if she could ride with her dad. Kristine said yes and then started filling her gas tank. When she was ready to go, Kristine waved to her husband and they resumed their trip.

At the next rest stop, Kristine was horrified to learn that Brooke was not with her husband (this was before cell phones). Her husband was completely surprised that Kristine expected Brooke to be with her. "I thought she was with you!" was the startled response from each. As quickly as they could, they found the number for the gas station they just left. Yes, their daughter was there, safe and waiting for them.

It turns out that after Brooke asked her mom if she could "ride with Dad," she went to the restroom. While Brooke was in the restroom, both cars drove away, each parent thinking that their daughter was in the other car. Both Kristine and Brooke laughed as they related this story to me, so all is forgiven.

One, two, three, four, five . . . looks like I'm not the only one working on that one!

[12]

When You Do Everything Right, And Yet-

SOMETIMES you do "everything right" as a parent and still your children are not model children; sometimes they even make serious mistakes. An experience I had in prison taught me that even when we try to do everything right, things can go dreadfully wrong.

One of the things I tried to do as an officer was to allow the inmates a little opportunity to save face. I reasoned that it was difficult for them to have a woman ordering them around. So, for example, after rec time when it was time for count, I would walk around and ask the inmates to return to the rooms for count time. But then I would walk away and give them a moment to complete their conversations. Generally speaking, the inmates seemed to appreciate this and they responded appropriately. There were some exceptions though.

One day, I asked one of the inmates, Hyde, to return to his cell. Then I walked away and continued asking other inmates to do the same. After I had made the rounds, I returned and Hyde was still standing in the common area. I said, "You need to go to your cell for count time. Now." This time I stood there and waited for him to comply. He didn't. I waited. He waited. "Go to your cell, or I'm going to write you up." He still refused.

In prison, officers can give inmates tickets for breaking the rules. When an inmate gets a ticket, they have to go to a disciplinary hearing. The consequences vary depending on the severity of the offense, the number of tickets the inmate has received, and whether or not he is going to see the parole board. They can range anywhere from a loss of privileges, a loss of a job, being moved to a higher security area of the prison, and so on.

So, I went to the control room and wrote Inmate Hyde a ticket. Another officer accompanied me to deliver it. Hyde refused to sign it, which didn't surprise us, and he finally went to his room for count time.

The next day, Hyde's friends tried to convince me to drop the ticket. They seemed very concerned for my welfare. I found this rather amusing. Since when did inmates care about what happened to officers? They claimed that he could make big trouble for me, but I was not phased. I assured them that as long as I followed the rules—and I had—there was nothing Hyde could do to get me in trouble with my superiors. I was wrong.

A couple of days later, I was called into the lieutenant's office. In prison, we use a military-type structure, so he was three levels up from me in rank. It was intimidating to be called to his office. I couldn't imagine what he could want. I went to his office and sat down. He made no small talk; he got straight to the point.

"We have some serious allegations against you from an inmate."

"What?" I said dumbfounded.

"Inmate Hyde has accused you of having sexual relations with him." The lieutenant then went on to tell me graphic details of what this inmate claimed had happened between him and me.

Shock and anger ignited within me. How dare he? Being very religious as I was (and continue to be) I was deeply offended on a personal level and a professional level. The accusation was unbelievable, unspeakable,and yet the lieutenant seemed to be taking it very seriously. How could this happen?

I did my best to explain what had happened with the ticket and the warning from Hyde's friends the following day. I assured the lieutenant that I never did the things he was accusing me of. His response was cold and unrelenting, "We will have to do an investigation. You should not talk to anyone about this." Then I was excused.

As I walked away from his office, I was in shock. How did this happen? I followed the rules. How could an inmate, a known rule-breaker by definition of the word, turn my world upside down with only a few words? And yet, so it was.

I was moved to a different cell block. Though I had been told not to talk to anyone about it, it quickly became evident that someone was talking. My officer friends from all over the prison asked me about it. Some even teased me, "Why would you do that for one of them and not for us?" Eeewww! Others said, "Don't worry, we know you didn't do it—you don't even swear!"

I felt like the woman with the Scarlet Letter. Sure, I knew my friends believed in me, but how many others thought it was true? The investigation dragged on and on. I kept asking when the investigation would be complete, but I only received excuses.

Finally, I had had enough. I was not a member of the union, but when one of the union members approached me and offered to help, I jumped at the offer. It was like having a bulldog attorney on my side. One of the union leaders coached me on the policy and procedure for "internal investigations." He explained that the investigation should be concluded within one month, and it had already been a month and a half. We made an appointment to see the lieutenant together.

With the help of my new friend from the union, the investigation was closed. The officials would not, however, proclaim me innocent. According to them, there was no proof either way. That still makes me fume. When there is no evidence, the benefit of the doubt should go to the officer, not to an inmate.

I tell you this story because unfortunately, as parents, sometimes things like this happen. You can do everything right and still have problems with your children. When that happens, parents lay awake looking for answers that will never come. Where did you go wrong? You didn't.

One of my church leaders, President David O. McKay, once said, "No success can compensate for failure in the home." I think many parents have used that statement to mentally lash themselves and deepen already serious wounds. I don't think that was Pres. McKay's intention at all though. I believe his point was that we should remember that our families are more important than careers or other worldly success, and we should devote our energies to them. He didn't mean that you are a failure if in spite of your best efforts, your children make disappointing choices.

As parents we can love, lead, guide, teach, cajole, but in the end children come with their own personalities and eventually make their own choices. Sometimes those mistakes will be minor and correctable, other times they are serious. I think about those inmates—all of them had mothers. I imagine that at least a few had good mothers. Mothers who are now asking themselves, "What more could I have done?"

I wish I had better answers for why sometimes things happen the way they do. The only thing we can do is to do the best we can. Then, at the end of the day, we must try to judge ourselves lovingly on the effort we put in and not the choices our children make.

Be kind to yourself, and be kind to fellow parents, because sometimes you can "do everything right" and things still go wrong

Index

LESLIE LIVES NEAR SEATTLE, WA with her husband, five children, and their dog. She likes reading, writing, and blogging. In addition to working full-time, she homeschools. The number one item on her bucket list is to "catch up on sleep."

CONTACT LESLIE:

Blog: Leslie's Illusions http://lesliegnelson.com
Healing from childhood abuse is like the scariest roller coaster you ever saw. Come raise your hands and scream with me. Here . . . we . . . go!

Twitter: http://twitter.com/lesliesillusion

Facebook http://facebook.com/lesliesillusions

Proof

Made in the USA
Charleston, SC
21 April 2014